Write and Sell Your Book

Mike Reuther

Published by Mike Reuther, 2023.

"I've had a sign over my typewriter for over 25 years now: Don't think!" – Ray Bradbury

Foreword

Is this you?

You've long wanted to write a book. I don't care what kind of a book.

Perhaps it's a military science fiction story, a romance, a western set in the late 1800s when the great American frontier was on the verge of vanishing.

You burn with a hot passion to write this story. It's been part of you for a long time. Driving to work in the morning, jacked on caffeine, you concoct scenes and characters to comprise this story. Maybe you think about this book during idle moments or while walking your dog or staring at meaningless numbers staring back at you on a computer screen in your work cubicle.

A day doesn't pass when you don't find yourself dreaming of this story or perhaps any number of stories and even, God forbid, of becoming an author.

Yes. You really think you would like to be an author.

Usually, you pass off these thoughts as silly notions. Writing a book? Becoming a writer? Why should you want to do that?

It's just not practical.

Sure. You can write. Maybe you got an A in that creative writing class you took as an elective back in college, but that was so long ago, before the marriage and the kids and the mortgage came along.

Write a book? Now?

When would you find the time? And how would you even start?

You can't think of one blessed person you know who's an author or even tried to write a book. For the love of all things practical, you're not a writer. Writers are misfits, oddballs, drunks, and drug addicts, most of whom end up penniless, alone, even suicidal.

Names such as Edgar Allen Poe and that guy who wrote Confederacy of Dunces come to mind. Even the great Ernest Hemingway, a writer you've longed admired, ended up killing himself.

It's quite easy to give up on a dream, any dream. We find ways to sabotage them with negative thinking. Why take a chance on something when we can remain true to our present existence, the haven of the familiar?

Writing a book is not easy, but it's not that hard either. At least, not as hard as you may think.

Like anything, the hardest part is getting started, deciding it's what you really want to do, and then finally putting yourself in front of that blank computer screen or piece of paper and writing.

Deciding you're going to do it. That is the hurdle to get over, the biggest barrier for anyone who longs to write a book.

In this book, you'll find inspiration. You'll get some tips and information from me, a guy who's been in the writing trenches for years as an author, journalist, and freelancer. I get into book marketing that is helpful too, although I don't wade deep into the weeds here as there are plenty of experts out there who can provide you with more detailed information in this area.

Maybe you've tried to write a book or two and given up. This book is for those writers as well. All authors hit a wall from time to time.

I hope to convey to you that writing a book really isn't that difficult. Like many things in life, it requires a certain amount of persistence and passion to do it well.

There's nothing magical about writing a book. Authors, with some exceptions, aren't these mad geniuses who climb rickety stairways to garrets, where they bang out their stories by candlelight on old Remington typewriters through the night while sipping on bourbon.

They don't venture into the dark woods on moonlit nights and gaze at that bright orb in the sky waiting for the muse to zap them with creative thoughts.

Writers come from all backgrounds and educational levels. Many are regular people, folks with day jobs and families, but with stories swirling in their heads they are dying to get out.

You too can write a book. In fact, you can write a lot of books.

Are you ready to try?

Keep reading. I guarantee you'll learn some things and hopefully be ready to take the plunge into the writing life.

The Evolution of a Writer

He was a twenty-something guy with dreams of becoming a writer.

He imagined writing that big book, that novel that would knock the socks off the literary world.

For a long time, striving to become a literary star remained just that—a dream.

Finally, after the twenty-something guy turned thirty, he decided it was time to put his dream into action, to start writing that book.

For two years, he scribbled away, furiously filling up notebooks in longhand.

Then one fine day, he went to the local post office and sent out his precious, typewritten manuscript, carefully bundled and packaged—his baby—to a literary agent in the great city of New York.

And waited.

Months later, the manuscript came back with a terse note about his work: Not for us.

He sent the manuscript or portions of it to other literary agents and waited but got pretty much the same unwanted response.

He wrote another book, and then another and another ...

Hungry to unlock the great secret for becoming a published writer, he studied Writers Market, the bible for writers, voraciously pored over the pages of Writer's Digest, a monthly guide for budding authors.

He no longer dreamed of being the next Hemingway. He just wanted published, to be able to call himself an author.

The years went by and there came many more rejection letters, all of which he filed away in a drawer. They would serve as reminders, he assured himself, of those many years when he could not get published.

Eventually, the writer found an agent. Finally, validation that someone believed in his work, his hard-earned reward for all the work and waiting and rejections.

Sadly, the agent couldn't find a place for his book.

Into his forties, he kept writing and sending out his manuscripts. It was the dawn of the internet age, and he no longer had to mail out chapters of his books and wait weeks or months for responses. Now, the rejections were coming by email, just hours after he sent out his queries.

And then, everything changed: The self-publishing era arrived.

No gatekeepers to prevent writers from publication. Finish a book and hit the publish button and Presto! you were an author.

But is that what he wanted? It seemed too easy, even wrong. All those years, writing and rewriting, earning his stripes to be an author, only to reach a time when anyone could be an author.

He was far from a young man now. All those years, all the rejections, yet somehow, he'd kept the faith, a foolish faith perhaps, a crazy chase of wasted days and nights that might have been better spent in another endeavor, something with a reward.

He was at a crossroads.

Maybe you can relate to this story, especially if you're an old baby boomer who pummeled those impenetrable doors of literary agents and publishing houses back in those halcyon days of the 1980s and '90s when life was slower and less complicated and it really did seem as if only the few, the anointed, became published authors.

Becoming a writer, let alone a successful one, is still no easy deal, and there remain agents and publishing houses that beckon writers with contracts, money and validation that they belong in the esteemed club of authors. Many still opt for this traditional publishing route and likely face what so many writers faced: rejection.

It's a choice every serious writer must eventually make, traditional publishing or self-publishing. I'll cover a bit more of the traditional versus self-publishing business later in the book.

Whatever choice you make, give the book your best effort. Write the book you want to write. Polish it, have it edited.

But don't stand on one book.

Write another book ... and another ... and another.

Grow as a writer. Improve. Get better.

Don't get frustrated. Okay. You will get frustrated, but if you really want to be a writer, you'll stay the course.

Let's See that Book

"What are you writing about?"

Has anyone ever asked you that question?

And if so, what was your reaction?

My guess is you felt a hint or huge wave of trepidation. It's a good bet you bit down hard on your lip, perhaps gave an embarrassed shrug, hesitant about revealing much if anything about your novel or other book in progress.

As writers, we tend to be close-mouthed about our work.

It's not that difficult to realize why.

Our books often represent our own longings or fears, our deep-seated feelings.

Someone asking to read the book we are writing can leave us sputtering: "No. No. It's only in the draft process, far from being close to finished."

Sharing our work with even a spouse or some other trusted or intimate acquaintance can be difficult.

Writers spend much of their days and evenings in their own heads, especially when writing fiction.

An author spilling heart and sweat and soul onto the pages of a book surely does not want that work to be dismissed or thought of as inferior.

You may well be one of those authors who has no problem sharing your words. You're not shy about having others in that writing group read, praise, and yes, even criticize your work.

But please, don't be one of those writers who spends years writing, rewriting, editing, and polishing a book only to keep it out of the hands of readers. Write the darn book and get it out there.

And then write another book and another.

It's what you've always wanted to do.

Am I right?

Finding the Kid Inside

If you're a writer, you should be a kid.

A kid? Really?

That's right.

Think about it.

When you were a kid the world was alive with possibilities. Everything was new, exciting, like going to the carnival or the circus.

You wanted to see everything and do everything.

It was a great feeling, one of euphoria, of rapturous delight.

You might not have always gotten what you wanted, but you felt sure that someday, somehow, you would ride that horse, hop aboard that boat out there on the water, or own that shiny toy in the store of that shop window.

As a kid, you were full of optimism, of delicious expectations.

Of course, we don't remain children.

We grow older, more realistic, even cynical, resigning ourselves to being adults and the responsibilities that come with being a mature, hardworking member of society.

Not that it's a bad thing but growing up can put a real crimp in our childhood imaginations that lifted us throughout our young lives.

Sometime, when you have nothing better to do, turn off the television, put away the cell phone, and close your eyes and think back to those days of your childhood.

Remember those moments, those experiences, when you felt particularly alive. What were you doing or what happened to you that has remained with you for so many years?

Maybe you carry fine memories of long, lazy days at your grandfather's farm, simply hanging out on the big wrap-around front porch with a perspiring glass of lemonade and gazing through the sunlight at the horses prancing about in the meadow. You fondly recall exploring the big old barn and jumping in the hay and its rich smell as you rolled about in it.

Do you remember the first fish you caught? Your best holiday memory?

The memories can be bittersweet or even painful too.

How about that first day of school when you were dropped off into a new world, a scary world away from home and the loving embrace of your family?

The point is not to necessarily write about scenes from your childhood, although you can certainly do that and come up with some fine stories, but to remember what it was like to be a kid, full of wonder and passion and feeling.

Use that wonder, that passion, that feeling in your own writing.

You'll be on the right track to successfully writing a book.

Start Writing Today

When is the right time to begin that longtime dream of writing a book?

Next week? This weekend?

After your son or daughter's soccer season ends?

Procrastination. It can be the death of a writer.

Many people who put off writing a book do so because they don't think they have the time.

Here's a little secret you probably already knew.

You must make the time, but it does not have to be an eight-hour-a-day session of pounding out prose on the keyboard. Sure, you can do it that way, and it can certainly work.

Let me suggest an easier, more manageable approach, especially if you're a newbie.

Find a spot in your day that you can use for writing. It certainly doesn't have to be a long amount of time. Block off two hours or less, five or six days a week for writing.

What's that? You say you have a busy life?

Many of us have busy lives.

Stop and think for a moment.

Is there time in your day that otherwise gets frittered away with checking your phone or social media sites, with staring at the television or other types of fruitless activities you can surely give up?

Perhaps every blessed minute of your day is taken up with important matters: working a full-time job, coaching a kids' team, cooking dinner, helping with homework. And that's just a regular day. How can I possibly, you ask, find time to write?

If you want to write, I mean, really want to write, you can find a way to do it.

Set your clock an hour earlier a few days a week so you can get out of bed and start writing that book. Maybe you can put aside some time before bed every night to write.

How about fifteen minutes in some part of your day?

Start out at fifteen minutes, perhaps three days a week. The point is to begin writing, even if it's just a little.

Don't wait until you retire, or the kids grow up or whatever, start writing—Now.

Maybe you don't feel good. Perhaps you're recovering from an illness, a physical, mental, or emotional problem. Maybe writing is just the activity you need to help you heal, to make you forget some of the problems of your life.

There may never be a best time to write a book. You may always find a reason to put off that dream. Ask yourself: How bad do I want to do it? Because, quite frankly, it does take a commitment to write a book.

Are you ready?

How Badly Do You Want to Write a Book?

Does writing a book absolutely consume you?

Is the need to write a book so overwhelming that you feel you will literally burst if you don't do it?

Perhaps you are already a writer but often find yourself stuck or blocked and you miss many days of writing. Do those unwriting days leave you feeling blue or angry?

Such feelings are not uncommon at all and are a sure sign that you really are a writer, that you should press on to become that author you always wanted to be.

So many of us are looking for fulfillment, to realize an ambition or a dream. Some burn to be an astronaut, a doctor, a champion figure skater, or successful business owner.

For the writer, it may be to pen the great American novel or the definitive book on some earth-shaking issue.

Your goals, of course, might be modest ones, but if the burning desire to write is there, chances are it's not going away. Perhaps you find yourself at age fifty awakened by a desire to write. You carried a flaming passion for writing at nineteen which you never fulfilled only to be stirred once again by these yearnings many years later.

Of course, it's never too late or too early to ignite those writing aspirations. You don't have to pass off the need to write as a silly daydream and the crazy thoughts of a mid-life crisis.

Don't think you're too young to write.

Hemingway and F. Scott Fitzgerald were mere lads in their twenties when they wrote their great novels.

Okay. Maybe you're not Hemingway or Fitzgerald. Perhaps you're not a genius.

But guess what? You don't have to be a genius.

The key to writing is to write, and to be you, putting down words in your natural voice, no matter your age, gender, race, or background.

Everyone has a story to tell.

Don't you think?

Getting in the Mood

Do you need to get in the mood to write?

How do you do it?

Do you turn on music? Drink coffee? Meditate?

Whatever works to put you into the flow, the rhythm of writing, is fine.

You see, there is no single trick to igniting one's writing. No one method is best or works for everyone.

Maybe you're a runner and find that works to clear your head before writing.

Many writers find it best to write first thing in the morning before the mind is cluttered with all kinds of unwanted thoughts and worries and concerns of the day. I recommend writing in the morning, the earlier the better, after a good night's sleep when the body and the mind are refreshed.

If you're just starting out as an author, chances are you have a day job or school or other responsibilities of life pulling at you and you have to squeeze in your writing time whenever you can.

Years ago, working as a news reporter and with family responsibilities, I used to steal away time during my lunch hour to write. Forget getting in the right frame of mind to write. I just did it, even when I didn't much feel like writing.

As a journalist, I had grown used to writing on deadline after rushing back to the newsroom. And really, that's all you must do when you sit down to write your book. You just do it.

Get those words down quickly, no matter how you feel before you begin every day. Writing a book should be something you do five, six, or even seven days a week, preferably at the same time each day.

Music, exercise, medication beforehand is fine if that's your ritual, if that's what fuels you.

But the real key is just doing it, finding that daily writing habit and sticking with it. Don't wait for the right moment or when you're in your Zen or the muse strikes you. Don't over-think and procrastinate, which for most authors are the two deadliest sins of all.

I Think I Want to be a Writer

I guess I first I set my sights on being a writer sometime around the fifth or sixth beer all those years ago, my mind running circles in an inebriated fog of possibilities.

Mad about literature, a devourer of books, a life stretched before me, my name one day emblazoned on the spines of books facing outward from some musty book shop of the future.

Ah yes. The intellectual life.

When you're eighteen or nineteen, and high on alcohol or drugs, anything seems possible.

You have your own dreams of being an author. Otherwise, you likely wouldn't be reading this book.

The question is: What are you doing about it?

Are you only dreaming the life of an author? For a dream to happen, inspiration must be accompanied by perspiration.

An idea, a creative burst will simply remain just that if not followed by the writing itself.

What are you doing to scratch that itch, that longing to be a writer? Are you sitting your derriere in that chair and putting down words?

If so, do you have a schedule, a regular time for writing?

Or is the thought of setting aside blocks of time to write everyday sound too much like a nine-to-five job, a gig you were hoping to avoid by becoming a writer in the first place?

Writing a book, make no mistake about it, requires some degree of discipline.

It's that daily writing routine that gets you into the rhythm, the momentum needed to finish that marathon for writing the book.

Make your writing dreams come true.

Get up tomorrow and knock off a few pages. Hell, a few paragraphs anyway.

Then repeat it the next day and the day after that.

A groundbreaking study done in the 1950s by Dr. Maxwell Maltz concluded that it can take a minimum of just 21 days to form a new habit.

Think about that.

Why not try on a new habit—the writing habit.

What have you got to lose?

How Do You Write?

How do you begin writing every day?

Does it take a cup of coffee to jumpstart your writing?

Are there certain rituals you go through before you write?

What sort of surroundings comprise your writing space?

Some authors simply would not think of writing without background music, perhaps burning incense or candles to capture just the right ambience to fuel the creative juices.

Maybe you don't need anything to help you along on your writing journeys. You can write anywhere.

For a time, I found New Age or soft music as just the right background for writing. But no music with lyrics lest I found myself singing the words in my brain and becoming sidetracked from the story.

How about a soundtrack that plays rushing water or falling rain or the whirring of a washing machine or dryer?

If you're a writer, you need to find your comfort zone and it's different for everyone.

Maybe you're just fine banging out words on a typewriter at the kitchen table. For someone else, the writing table is a door across some cinder blocks in a garage.

The great novelist Thomas Wolfe wrote in longhand standing up. Jack Kerouac banged out his classic novel, On the Road, on scroll paper.

Books have been written from jail cells and mental institutions. The Diary of Anne Frank was created by a Jewish teenage girl hiding from the Germans during World War II.

What have you got to say? What book do you want to write?

If the will to write is there, you won't need the music, the burning candles, the computer with all the best book-writing software.

You'll just write the darn book.

Some budding authors wait till November rolls around for NaNoWriMo otherwise known as National Novel Writing Month.

NaNoWriMo is the annual creative writing project in which participants attempt to write a 50,000-word manuscript between Nov. 1 and Nov. 30. For many writers, it's a great way to jump-start that book dying to get out.

But you don't have to wait for Nov. 1 to come around. Pretend today is NaNoWriMo and start writing.

Launching Pads for Writing

One day at dusk, as I left one of my favorite fishing spots, I spotted a tree.

It might have been a maple, perhaps an oak.

What caught my attention was the color, the autumnal splendor of this tree in the waning sunlight of an early November day.

There it was before a cabin amidst the mountains of northcentral Pennsylvania, like a lemon drop upon a stem, its leaves a burst of brilliant yellow.

I tried to take a picture of this tree, just as I described it, but being the amateur photographer that I am, and with nothing other than a cellphone camera to capture this natural wonder, the photo came out dark.

But I expect the tree will remain in my memory.

Perhaps I'll use that tree in some future writing project.

Those images we encounter in everyday life can serve as springboards to the imagination.

Perhaps that tree was planted many years ago by a man to honor a beloved son who lost his life in the roiling waters of that nearby trout stream. Maybe the tree is a matter of dispute between two landowners on bordering properties and is in danger of being cut down.

Imagine there was a treehouse in that tree that holds some forbidden secrets of children, now grown, who used it as a hideaway where they engaged in strange rituals.

Pick out an object, any object, and your mind can take flight, devising stories, wonderful tales that should be told.

Sit in a park or an airport and watch people go by.

What about that man in the suit and tie sitting all alone, staring out the window of a commuter train looking forlorn? Did he just lose his job as part of some mass wave of furloughs? What's his story? What will happen to him?

As writers, we are fortunate to have this vast world surrounding us. There are a million stories to tell, and it's quite easy to launch a novel, a short story, if we just get out of our own way and let our minds wander.

When it Isn't Happening

Is it possible to write pages and pages of a book only to find out that the story you launched all those weeks ago just is not working?

Yes.

It's happened to me. It's happened to many authors.

That novel you were so passionate about somehow gets away from you or just isn't going the way you had hoped.

It's great to write and go on a journey and not know exactly where the story is taking you, but sometimes a story can seem to come to a dead end.

The characters no longer resonate or the flow of the writing seems to disappear and you find yourself spending more time staring at the computer screen with your fingers resting on the keyboard instead of tapping madly away upon it.

And then ... you're checking social media sites or your emails and not writing at all.

No writer likes the idea of giving up on any project. All that time spent writing only to toss it all away seems like such a waste.

There is nothing at all wrong stepping away from a story that isn't working. It comes with being an author.

Then again, don't be so quick to kill it from your laptop or burn the pages in the fireplace. Perhaps you can return to the book some day.

Pausing a project that simply leaves you blocked or frustrated is fine, but it may be salvageable. Months or even years later, you could pull that unfinished manuscript from a drawer, dust it off and resurrect it.

Beyond that, don't stop writing after one book leaves you defeated. Go on to something else.

Too many writers left stymied by one book give up on writing altogether.

Remember. There are plenty of stories to be told and with imagination and the will to do it, you can be the author who writes a few of them.

Stumped What to Write

Are you stumped about what to write?

Do you figure everything that's ever been written has been done and put to rest for the ages?

Well ... consider this. You are your own voice. You are unique with something to say, maybe even something quite important to say to the world.

Sure, the plight of mankind and what human creatures are doing here on this planet has been written to death. Science fiction stories of every kind have been put to paper. Obscure figures who come from nowhere to emerge as mythic heroes have been made into best-selling novels.

And yet, your story, the way you might want to present some similar narrative, can be told as well.

You see, we really are all different in so many ways. There are countless ways to tell a story, and everyone has their own writing style and slant on things.

Each of us has experiences and backgrounds that we can draw from in writing these wonderful books. There is always room for more stories out there, and readers eager to devour them.

That goes for nonfiction as well.

You see, it's *how* you write the story. After all, there is no one like you. Give yourself a chance. If you have that burning desire to write whatever it is inside you, you owe it to yourself to do it.

Now, what's stopping you?

A Bit about Marketing

If you're just starting out in self-publishing with dreams of being successful, you may have already encountered some of the stumbling blocks of the writing life.

You likely learned that after publishing your novel or non-fiction book for all the world to see, your real work commenced.

You want people to read your book and, of course, spend their hard-earned money on it.

What most newbie authors painfully learn is that the sales don't come rolling in once they publish. There are literally millions of books out in the marketplace and the chance of many people finding your magnum opus is slim.

What to do?

Well ... what you'll likely do is spend an inordinate amount of time, likely more time than is emotionally healthy, searching and scanning the internet for the best and most cost-effective means of marketing and promoting your book.

And boy oh boy, will you find the sites out there, countless of them, making claims their marketing tool is the single magic bullet for selling thousands of copies of books. Most won't work, and it's a good bet you'll question why you ever decided to write in the first place.

I've made my share of mistakes with marketing, including shelling out money for book promotion sites that brought me little or nothing in return.

Before you go out and spend more dollars than you can afford to market your book, make sure you first have all your ducks in a row.

Write a good book, free as possible of grammar and spelling errors. Don't be afraid to spend just a little bit for a good editor or proofreader.

Make sure it has an eye-catching cover. Yes, a cover is important, and there are plenty of talented graphic artists out there to create one for you without hitting you hard in the pocketbook.

Do a little research on keyword strategies which help people find your book more easily.

Check out some social media sites on writing where other authors gather and share their concerns. It's a good place to find out what's happening out there, and what works and doesn't work in self-publishing.

Find out who the real experts are in self-publishing. Check out their books or their YouTube sites.

One of the more informative and best self-publishing gurus, at least in my humble opinion, is Dale L. Roberts, who has site called Self-Publishing with Dale. He's an author with countless YouTube productions on a variety of topics covering the self-publishing world.

Meanwhile, keep writing. Get out that next book and the next one after that.

After all, you're a writer.

I will go into marketing tactics later in this book. I promise. Keep reading.

The Magic Cards

You're not sure what story you want to write.

Those idle moments you spend sitting on the front porch after dinner make your mind wonder. Those cups of coffee in the morning fuel a frenzy of story possibilities.

So many ideas are shooting through your brain that you think you might go crazy.

Just stop a minute.

Countless ideas for books are a good problem for an author. Maybe all those ideas add up to multiple books or just one really great book or story.

Try the magic cards. It's the method I've used to launch the writing of my own books.

The process is quite simple. I sit with the cards, pen in hand, and simply scribble out a word or a few words of images or thoughts that come to me. After a half hour, perhaps longer, I have dozens, even hundreds of words and phrases on those cards.

Later, I go through all the cards and see what I have. Usually, it's a rough outline of a book.

Don't get me wrong. I don't use all the ideas that I randomly scribble down, but I certainly have created a road map for a book.

Of course, you don't have to feel constricted by the cards to write your book. You'll almost certainly come up with more ideas. I've found the cards to be an incredible way of freeing up those apprehensions and fears I get before starting a book.

Try it.

Do it quickly, jotting down those words on the cards the very moment they come into your brain. It's quite likely that the book you've been wanting to write for so long was just dying to come pouring out. The cards are perfect for finally capturing what will go into the book—setting, characters, conflict, the very essence of the story.

Don't look at this exercise as a chore. Be in a relaxed state when you write on those cards. Basically, it's allowing the subconscious to take over. If you don't want to use cards, bang out words and phrases on your laptop.

That works too.

Rules for Writing? Well ... Maybe One

I always like to say there are no hard-fast rules for writing a book.

However, there may be one.

Here it is: Start out a book with a hook, a means of sparking interest in your readers.

We all know the best means of losing a reader is by beginning with the timeworn, Once upon a time ...

If you're writing a mystery, don't be afraid to introduce the murder, the dead body in the first chapter, if not the first page.

Who is the most interesting character of the book and why? What is this person after and why?

Make the reader immediately want to know more about this character and what he or she wants.

Maybe you use your first chapter to describe some place, a haunted mansion high atop a mountain where strange events occur, and people vanish.

Building suspense is fine, but you don't have to wait till chapter six for your story to take off.

Think of the books that kept you interested.

Why did you keep reading? And I'm not talking about books you had to read for a high school or college literature class.

Chances are the story grabbed you at the outset and made you want to continue turning the pages.

Slap readers awake with a great first sentence like this one from Harry Potter and the Philosopher's Stone: "Mr. and Mrs. Dursely of number four, Privet Drive, were proud to say that they were perfectly normal, thank you very much."

Kind of makes you want to read on. Right?

There's nothing worse than a boring story, and there's no sure-fire way to lose a reader than to start out a book with humdrum details or a long narrative that rambles or meanders.

Sure, some writers can pull this off with a unique approach, say provocative description or lyrical prose that touches the very soul of the reader. As I mentioned before, there are no hard-fast rules, and I don't mean to contradict myself.

I think of all the times I've clicked on the purchase button of an Amazon Kindle ebook after reading through just the first chapter or so of the story. The books I don't buy or download or the ones that don't quickly grab my attention.

Whatever you write, put forth your best effort, but special attention should be given to the very beginning of your book.

In journalism, students are taught to get the who, what, where, why and how of a story in that first paragraph. The story then flows from there.

Don't be afraid your story will lose its impact if you start it out with something dramatic or altogether interesting, lest you burn up your best material right away.

You might be surprised how much easier it is to write your book when you start it out with a bang.

Whatever the Weather

One day not long ago, as I was sitting at my computer, I happened to notice the wind blowing clumps of February snow from the branches of the trees in the forest outside my window.

I love the wind.

I like the sound it makes, especially on a late fall or winter day, rustling the bare branches, howling sometimes like the cry of an invisible creature from the distance.

There is something comforting about a healthy gale and a blustery day or night.

Don't you think?

Maybe it's because it makes me forget some of the troubles of the world, a reminder that when we really get down to it, nature is in control.

If nothing else, I can imagine one of those bursts of wind carrying me off to some place of the imagination.

A windy March day, a summer rain, snowflakes gently falling, can be springboards for our creative bursts. They can serve as backgrounds to the stories we create and add to the element of suspense or mystery or the very mood of the books we write.

The weather is an effective element of any story.

A sun-splashed June day can paint a happy scene, perhaps a couple in love strolling along a beach. Pounding rain can set a different tone, perhaps foreshadowing the doom of a character.

When it comes to the weather, it's easy to just surrender to the imagination.

Many of us do it all the time without realizing it.

Clouds and drizzle greeting us on a November day are a downer, a grim warning of a bad day at work.

Bright sunshine illuminating the colors of autumn bring smiles and hope, gearing us up for a drive in the country, perhaps a walk in the woods.

Writing, especially that of fiction, should be about surrendering to emotions to evoke the images, the very feel of the story.

The weather can play a big part to set the scenes of your own book.

Don't ignore the weather.

It's a powerful ingredient to mix into any story and part of writing from the heart rather than from the brain.

Let Your Emotions Guide Your Writing

It's the morning after the big presidential election.

Emotions are running high.

As I write this, an historic election has not been settled.

There are people on both sides of the political spectrum wondering: Why didn't everyone vote for my candidate? Didn't the message resonate?

Or even: How can so many people be so stupid, so blind?

I raise this issue because the election to decide who leads the greatest nation in the free world has been an emotional one, a kind of wakeup call for people across the nation for many months.

Let's face it. Politics, for better or worse, emanate strong feelings.

If you're an author looking for something to write about, there may be no better topic. I'm not suggesting you launch a book about your hatred or love for a certain politician or ideology. On the other hand, it's not a bad topic for a book.

My point is you can find a subject that stirs you, that brings out feelings deep within your soul, an issue that angers, saddens, or raises scalding hot tears to drip down your face. A topic of which you feel so strongly that you are bursting inside like a volcano ready to explode.

There exists no shortage of things to write about in this big wide world of ours. Life itself is complex, often with no easy answers.

A writer can explore these questions through essays or columns or even a short story or novel.

You say you don't know what to write about?

Think again.

You Are Unique

There is a great song by The Byrds, I Was Not Born to Follow.

The song is part of the cult classic film, Easy Rider, which follows the story of two bikers in those tumultuous days of the late 1960s who follow their own path in life only to ultimately meet their doom.

The message that you should meet others' expectations and standards hits us over the head every day—in our workplaces, in advertising, among our friends and acquaintances.

It's easy to go with the norm, to conform to standards.

Many writers are no different. They try to copy other authors, mimicking their prose style, their stories.

But here's the thing: Everyone is unique.

Every author who has ever sat down before a keyboard brings something different to the table, from their past experiences, backgrounds, and inner lives.

There is no cookie-cutter mold for writers. Nor should there be.

If you are just starting out as a writer, don't try to emulate other authors. Write what you want to or must write. And do it in your own voice and style.

When you write, you should only try to please one person—you. Not your friends, not the people in your writing group, not even that eighth-grade English teacher who said you'd never be a writer.

Writing with honesty can mean taking a leap of faith. Then again, anything worth doing often demands that jump into the unknown.

If you want to write and are dying to tell a story, you need to simply do it.

Forget the hang-ups, those voices that nag at you with the words that you can't do it.

Dismiss the fears and start writing—in your own voice.

Procrastination is only time lost.

Again, everyone is unique.

Be true to yourself and you'll find your way as a writer.

Find Your Passion

What book do you want to write?

Here's the thing.

To sit down and commit yourself to banging away on a keyboard two hours a day or more, you need to enjoy the process.

If you are just starting out on this writing journey and looking for the best ways to make money, you will most surely come across advice about targeting markets.

I'm talking, of course, about what kind of book will sell.

Mysteries and romances have long been popular genres. There are countless subgenres that readers devour as well. I can't say it's wrong to target a popular genre. Many writers are doing quite well knocking off series of books and collecting legions of readers along the way.

I'm not going to tell you that writing to market makes a writer a sellout.

This whole writing gig is a tough racket and far be it from me to criticize anyone who wants to make money, perhaps lots of money, from their labors. We're all different.

My dream early on was to write contemporary fiction about people, real people, not aliens or Hobbit creatures from Middle Earth or ghosts or grizzly creatures that haunt or stampede villages.

I wasn't interested in foreign espionage, apocalyptic, end-of-time stories, or other flights of fantasy that take me to other worlds or dimensions.

Not that there is anything wrong with those types of books. They're just not my cup of tea. I never bothered reading any of those types of stories, so why would I want to try and write them?

If fire-breathing dragons or covens of witches or time travel or God knows what other types of stories jazz you up, then by all means, write those books. Otherwise, write what you want to write. Write what excites you or scares you or brings you to tears. It doesn't matter.

The more passion you bring to your writing every day, the better your story will be.

Believe me.

Better yet. Believe in yourself, to write that story burning inside you.

Do You Like to Write?

"Do you like to write?" the professor asked as he stood before the classroom of Journalism 101 university students.

As one, we nodded our assent.

"I hate it," he responded with a wry grin. "But I have to write."

This bearded tall man explained how he had to always be busy writing something—a magazine article, an academic piece.

It wasn't that he liked to write, it's that he had to write.

I often think about the words spoken by that teacher so many years ago.

I appreciated his honesty, but I also wondered if he should have been imparting such wisdom to young somewhat impressionable students, many of whom would soon embark in careers as reporters.

Would it have been better for him to tell us how "fun and exciting" writing can be, how it can send our souls soaring to new heights.

Perhaps he was trying to weed out those who really didn't have their hearts into writing, who weren't willing to put the blood and sweat into their writing. Writing can surely be hard, and yes, there are many days when the words don't come tumbling out of us.

I write fiction, but I've made a living for many years as a journalist, writing plenty of articles I had to write, instead of pieces I wanted to write.

I suppose what the professor was trying to impart to us was that this whole business of writing, any kind of writing, is a tough racket.

It isn't for dreamy-eyed souls tapped gently on the head by muses who inspire them to compose lyrical prose. On the other hand, writing doesn't have to be a grind, especially if it's not your day job.

Make it a passion. Find what you want to write.

Write the book you want to write, not what someone else wants you to write.

Life is short. Write your way.

Skiing Is Like Writing

Not long ago, I took a ski lesson.

Call it a successful check-off on my long list of bucket list items.

I had been on skis before, but only a few times to do some cross-country skiing.

I wasn't sure quite what would happen if I attempted to go down a hill. I'm not a young man, and I have a trick knee from a long-ago football injury.

I was apprehensive, to say the least. I didn't want to tear up my knee, break my bones, or perhaps kill myself.

To sum up, I did okay, aside from getting off that stupid ski lift.

Alright, I admit, I managed to go from the top of a snow-covered gentle rise to the bottom—the beginner's slope.

Our teacher stood below us, yelling out instructions, pointing his hand one way and then the other.

And really, that's all there was to it. Like a bandleader conducting his musicians, he led us zigzagging down that hill.

I was in this rhythm descending that incline.

Good writing is like that.

When you get into a rhythm, the words flow.

That rhythm comes from writing every day, preferably the same time every day, sitting down at the computer or before that tablet and just letting the words come.

If you continue writing and don't give up, you'll become better at it.

You may stumble in your writing, just as I am sure to stumble and even fall if I continue with skiing and even take on bigger hills to descend. Heck, I'll probably fall flat on my face a few more times just getting off the ski lift.

Practice makes perfect, to borrow a time-worn cliché. But of course, it's true.

Find your rhythm and the writing comes more easily, like snowflakes gently falling from the sky.

A Single Idea Sparks a Story

Take an idea, any idea, and start writing.

It's all you need for a story.

Your intuition knows what to write, so get out of the way.

That's advice from the late great science fiction author and storyteller Ray Bradbury.

So, what does it mean?

Don't over-think when you write. Go with your heart, your gut.

When you begin a book, it's easy to fall into that practical, left-brain mode of overthinking.

Maybe you know the drill.

Okay. I have a great idea, but where do I go from there and how about the next chapter and the one after that ... and what if this book doesn't work. My God. This is overwhelming. I can't write a book.

Slow down. Don't panic. Don't trip before you take that first step.

Just go with the flow.

Let me repeat that: *Just go with the flow.*

Much of life requires us to plan and organize what we do. And that's fine. It would be difficult to get through our daily lives if we didn't.

And you can write that way, in a cautious, plodding manner. You can outline a book, detail every chapter, do character sketches out the kazoo.

God knows, many writers go about writing a book this way, and it isn't necessarily wrong.

But there is a better way.

Do you know what it is?

Get the words down fast, let the writing determine where the book goes.

Here's the thing. It's likely when you sit down to write that magnus opus, you had a pretty good idea what you wanted to say anyway.

Trust your instincts. You'll be surprised what happens when you turn on that spigot and let the words flow.

What you write won't be perfect. So what?

First drafts of books never are perfect. Then again, neither are eighth, ninth and tenth drafts.

There will be time for reflection, for editing, to go back and fix those parts of the book that don't work.

Make writing a book a journey, not an arduous task.

Write fast. Write from the heart.

Being Your Own Worst Critic

One of the biggest hang-ups for writers is the fear of not being good enough.

Too many authors, and I'm talking mostly about those writing their first book, are afraid that anything they write will be lousy, garbage, not worth anyone's time.

The common feeling is: Who will ever want to read what I write?

They defeat themselves before they even get out of the starting gate.

Are you feeling that way?

If so, get over it.

Don't let negativity rule your life.

You really don't have to write like Hemingway or Stephen King or some other famous author, especially when you are a newbie.

In any type of career or endeavor, there is a starting point. Few of us are great or even good at something when we just start out.

Don't give up on your writing when it seems as if you're failing, when the words looking back at you on the computer screen appear to be the mere scribblings of the worst amateur.

What you wrote probably isn't as bad as it seems to you. After all, everyone is their own worst critic.

And even if your writing needs work, so what?

You've gambled nothing. You've done nothing more than invest time in a learning process.

Sit yourself down the next day and write again. Then keep writing for more days.

Don't look at writing as Sisyphus pushing a boulder up a hill for eternity. The good writing days will come.

Practicing your craft (and yes writing is a craft) will make you better.

Do not give up.

Keep at it.

Maybe you won't write lyrical prose like Faulkner or compose sentences that sing to the Gods.

Here's a tip.

The most successful writers aren't necessarily the ones with the most talent. They are the ones who work the hardest at their craft.

They write five, six, seven days a week.

They don't wait for the muse to come calling, for inspiration to hit them.

Believe it or not, they likely suffered through the same doubts about their writing, perhaps contemplated or even gave up, only to return to what they were meant to do—write.

How about you?

Hitting a Wall

It's those frustrating times that really test a writer, those days when you really don't feel like putting yourself in front of a keyboard and pounding out words.

Maybe it's because the writing has become difficult.

Perhaps you feel the futility of it all.

You may know what I mean.

No one is ever going to care what I write. What do I have to say that is unique or bold or interesting? Who am I to write a book about anything?

Unless you are one of those rare souls eager to jump out of bed and write every single blessed day for the rest of your life, you are going to have those times.

Momentum is such an important part of being a writer. Showing up every day to do the writing is half the battle.

And guess what?

When you show up and put yourself before that blank page and commence the process of writing, you often get back into the flow.

Giving up is easy.

But instead of collapsing to the floor and crumpling into a ball in surrender, you must ask yourself how badly you want to write. How long have you wanted to become an author?

Think of all those days you spent wondering if you could ever take that giant leap into becoming an author. Think of the regret that will hound you if you simply walk away from something you wanted to do for longer than you can remember.

Years ago, when I hit a wall with my own writing, I did just that. I quit.

I took a course in real estate and got my license. I had already spent years trying to sell my books to literary agents not interested in my books. Why not? I thought, change the course of my life.

In the back of my mind, I felt I would eventually go back to the writing, but it seemed I needed a break from the writing.

Well, to make a long story short, as they say, selling houses didn't exactly work out for me.

I gave up real estate, returned to the keyboard, and finished a novel I had started before veering off into that other venture.

If you're burning to write and become an author, chances are the feeling won't abandon you for good.

There is a good chance you will hit a wall at some point with your writing. You'll put heart and soul into your writing and smack up hard against that wall.

Don't sweat it.

Go right back to the keyboard and do what you were meant to do.

You may ask yourself why you should write a book when you can do something else with your time.

It's then you have to ask yourself why you wanted to become an author. What drove you to the keyboard to knock off words?

Do you consider it a hobby?

There's nothing wrong with taking up writing as a hobby. Nothing at all. But I suspect if you're reading this book, you want to take your writing beyond some fun activity or diversion.

It does take a commitment to do it well, and that means showing up to do the writing. I'm not talking eight hours a day, but one or two hours a day anyway.

Don't play the comparison game. Don't fall into the trap of thinking you can't write, or at least, not write as well as Tom or Sue, those hotshot people in your writing group, who have published several books or more apiece.

So, what if Tom writes heart-stopping lyrical prose and Sue has quit her job down at the library thanks to the skyrocketing sales on Amazon of her romance fiction.

The comparison game is bad stuff, in all phases of life. It's better to be you and write what you want to write and take advantage of your own unique talents than look around to see what everyone else is doing.

There's room for all sorts of writers, with all kinds of voices and things to say to the world.

Don't lose sight of why you are writing and why you want to do it.

Ask yourself how you'll feel if you do quit writing. I can answer that for you: Miserable.

Need a break from writing? Go ahead and take a break. Just beware that it's difficult to start up again, and that goes with just about anything when you take that a holiday from it.

We all want validation in life, authors need it like anyone else. Putting yourself in front of the computer every day, all alone, to bang out words, is not easy. It does take a certain amount of discipline and desire to keep at it.

I know. I've been doing it for more years than I can count, while still holding down a full-time job at a newspaper where I write more stories.

I fell in love with fiction and the written word in my youth. I slowly came to the realization after reading books that I too wanted to try and become an author.

I suppose I had the optimism of youth, that perhaps the literary Gods would reach down and anoint me as the voice of my generation. Lofty thoughts? Sure.

But sustaining any dream requires a certain amount of crazy thinking. Don't you think?

Maybe you have the talent to compose the sort of prose that sings to the heavens. You've won countless writing contests since junior high, but now you've decided to really get serious with your talent and start writing those books you were meant to write.

Great.

But don't put your talent on cruise control and think that alone will zoom you to the top of best-seller lists by the end of this year. You'll still have to put that fanny down in the chair and do the work.

That's what it takes, and just like the less talented wordsmiths out there struggling in their initial efforts to write, you'll become better at your craft if you practice it.

Writing is like other endeavors. Practice may not make perfect—nothing does—but it certainly leads to improvement.

I Don't Have Time to Write

Most of us must make a living.

Money doesn't fall from the sky. We need to work for it, and that means holding down a job, often a job that requires a lot of time.

A big reason many people decide not to write is because they feel they simply don't have the time, or even energy after putting in a long day's work. Many people in today's economy hold down two or even three jobs.

Who wants to do anything but turn on the TV and stare at it like a zombie watching the pictures zip by after putting in a tough day on the docks or pouring over countless reports in a cubicle?

Of course, if you really want to write, you'll find it within yourself to perhaps write anyway. Making the writing a priority is the key.

Let's say you really do want to write. You hate your job. Or, perhaps you don't hate it, but see it as nothing more than a means of earning money to put food on the table and a roof over your head. You're not looking to climb the corporate ladder. That nine-to-five job certainly isn't your passion.

You might consider finding work that fits more into your schedule to allow you to chase that author dream.

Are you willing to quit that job, the one that pays you rather handsomely to pursue the goal?

Most people aren't willing to take such risks, to give up good jobs in pursuit of dreams.

What about you?

There are many types of jobs, including ones that are almost perfect for writers.

How about becoming a security guard? It's an easy gig for the most part. I worked in a brewery warehouse as a security guard for a time and managed to do quite a bit of writing on the job.

I made my checks going through the factory several times a night before coming back to my station. The building was quiet on the swing or midnight shift, and I was left with nothing to do but stare out the window looking out at the mostly empty parking lot.

Instead, I wrote. When I got tired of writing, I pulled out a book and did some reading. And we all know, reading is an activity all writers should be doing.

How about sales? A lot of people cringe at the thought of pushing insurance or other products at people, coming up against deadlines and quotas.

There are plenty of sales jobs out there. For many sales jobs, it's making your calls, checking emails, doing follow-ups, and the rest of your day is free. Unless you're in a high-pressure type of work situation, a sales job can allow a lot of time for writing.

In real estate, a realtor isn't even considered an employee, but a contracted worker. Realtors come and go as they please, making their calls, showing homes. No need to report to the office every day. That kind of flexible schedule is perfect for a writer.

These are just two jobs that can work for a writer. There are others. You can walk dogs, do house sitting. The list is endless.

You can, of course, hold down a demanding job and still write.

Scott Turow worked as a lawyer in Chicago and wrote on the train during his commutes into the city. He persisted and ended up becoming a best-selling author.

Such perseverance, drive and energy may be beyond many of us, but it's evidence that writing a book can be done under difficult, even trying circumstances.

How badly do you want to write?

If the desire is there, you'll find a way to get the writing done.

Nothing will stop you.

Take care of yourself. Get your exercise and avoid the bad habits that can spell doom—heavy drinking or drugs. The more energy you have, the more you'll be willing and able to take on the challenge of writing a book.

It's part of getting in the right frame of mind to make the dream happen.

What Do You Want to Write?

I still hold down a full-time job as a newspaper reporter while continuing to write books. At 63 years young, I'm no spring chicken.

I've kept at it a long time. I've written novels, short stories, and of course, books on writing like this one you are now reading. I like to share my experiences and help others realize their own dreams of becoming authors.

You likely have a book in you that is dying to get out, just as I did when I sat down one night many years ago and began writing my first novel, scribbling out the words in a notebook. Writing is like an itch that simply must be scratched.

What do you want to write?

Perhaps you want to write about yourself, your life, or a fictional memoir. You have experiences that you simply must share with the world, maybe a triumph over some tragedy or mistake.

Maybe all those mysteries you read in your spare time have inspired a desire to create your own hard-boiled sleuth and cases he or she solves.

How about a funny novel? There was that telemarketing job you held down for a while. The work sucked, but it sure would make for an interesting novel with its cast of eccentric characters, office politics, and miserable working conditions.

Maybe you want to make a difference in the world with your book. Pick a topic. There are plenty of them. The environment. Politics. Health care. Poverty. Saving the whales.

Using your writing to chronicle the ills of society and a call for action can make a great book. Beyond that, it can impassion you.

Over my long career as a journalist, I've found there is nothing quite like a pat on the back, a kind word from a reader who liked that article you wrote on some important topic that needed to be written about.

Passion and desire are such an important aspect of the writing process and crucial for fueling an author and building the momentum to keep the words flowing each day. It can make it fun too.

What about something you know a lot about? Maybe you have expertise in some activity or line of work that you'd love to share with others.

Again, it can be on just about any topic.

Get those magic cards out and brainstorm. Watch a story come alive.

Persistence

I like to inspire writers, give them hope, because I know how tough it can be to write a book.

I'm not referring now so much about the process of writing itself. I'm talking about those long hours you spend away from the writing, when the self-doubts creep in, when you wonder if this whole business of putting yourself in front of the keyboard every day will ever come to anything.

CBS This Morning recently featured an author named Steven Pressfield who found success with his book, The Legend of Bagger Vance, and other works. But Pressfield's journey was far from an easy one.

He spent many years writing before making any kind of money at all. He worked odd jobs, crisscrossed the county, became a kind of nomad. He got depressed, thought about giving up, wondered what it all meant. He was well into middle-age before he found success.

He didn't give up. He had a dream and he stayed true to it.

His story is not altogether unusual.

Imagine going through a life and not trying to realize a dream. You don't want to go to your death bed with regrets.

Perhaps making money or becoming a best-selling author are not your goals. And that's fine. But to realize any kind of success is going to take some work, some time, and yes, no little bit of persistence.

But then again, persistence is required to make it in any field of endeavor.

In the movie, The Founder, there is a scene early in the film where Ray Kroc, who found crazy success with McDonald's restaurants, is listening to a self-improvement record. The gist of the message is that talent, genius, education are not the keys to success. Rather, it's persistence.

Find your own persistence. Tape the word to the wall of your writing room. Stare at it each day before you begin writing.

Don't give up.

People will discourage you from your writing, if not question your reasons for wanting to be a writer. They'll pass of your dreams of being an author to youthful craziness, a mid-life crisis, or some other reason. Some people might be jealous that you found passion, something you want to do.

Sure. There will also be those who have your back, and their kind words will be supportive. But it's you who will do the writing. Just you. You'll often feel alone because you will be alone, writing down words, creating.

No one, save another writer, will completely understand why you're spending all that time in a room closed off from everyone. And that's okay. Deflect the negativity. Stay positive.

Keep writing.

What is Your Goal as an Author?

The most financially successful writers are those who know how to market.

It's a bitter pill for many authors to swallow.

People scribble away on pads and bang away on keyboards turning out wonderful stories. And yet, more times than not, these talented writers remain obscure and anonymous with little to show for their efforts other than perhaps the admiration of peers.

I throw this out there as a warning.

It's fine to want to write but beware that it's not the most talented or even hardworking writers who grab the brass ring.

If you're new to this whole business of becoming an author, take a step back for a moment and think what you want to do with your writing.

What is your end goal?

To simply write a book? To make a difference? To make money?

If the goal is to make money, you can look forward to spending oodles of time promoting your book. And even then, you might not see much of a return.

There exist countless ways to market books, from using Facebook ads to email marketing.

Some self-published authors learn how to successfully market while many others who seek to make a living from their books fail miserably at marketing.

What about you?

Again, is writing a book the end goal? Or are you looking to make money too?

Think about it.

Preparing Your Book

If you are just starting out as an author with visions of selling books by the boatload and earning hundreds and thousands, even millions of dollars, take a deep breath.

I want to dissuade you of that crazy notion.

It is possible to become a best-selling author and live in a beachside home in Malibu and rub shoulders with the beautiful people and appear on CNN yakking up your latest magnum opus.

But for most of us, and surely for those of you just starting out as authors, a reality check is in order.

You don't just write a book, hit the publish button and ... presto ... tons of buyers will download your book on Amazon. It doesn't work that way.

Many of you perhaps know better.

You don't have your head up there in the clouds, blinded by the notion of crazy fantasies of movie deals and mega-mansions. You just want to write the best book you can possibly write, and yes, make some money too.

If you're a self-published author and you want to see some kind of earnings from your books, you must start thinking like a businessperson.

I know. You want to write and leave the advertising, the promotion to others.

Unfortunately, there are many people out there feeding off writers, waiting to take your money without following through to do a good job promoting your books.

Be careful how you spend money on marketing.

Take baby steps, do your research, find out the best ways to advertise. After all, you spent a lot of time writing a book.

Do some comparison shopping.

Look at YouTube and other free online sites and check out what seasoned authors have to say.

However, before you start spending any money on marketing, prepare the successful groundwork.

Get an attractive cover.

You may have written a page-turner, but if potential readers don't like the way it looks, they most likely won't buy it. People really do judge a book by its cover.

Write a solid description for your book. There are countless sites on how to write book descriptions that attract readers, or you can find someone to write one for you, often without breaking the bank.

Getting reviews for your book is always helpful. After all, potential readers want to know what others think of a book before they buy it.

These are some of the very basics of preparing a book for publication that I'll cover later.

Writing a book and successfully marketing it and quitting the day job, if that's your goal, can happen, but it doesn't happen overnight.

Be patient. Stay the course. Do your homework.

If you've written a book, congratulations.

Selling it is the next big step.

You've Written Your Book ... Now What?

You've written your book, hopefully polished it and had it proofread and edited. You're looking forward to publishing it through Amazon, Draft2Digital, Smashwords or any of the other self-publishing platforms out there.

You are eager not only to have people read it, but to sell some copies of your fantastic novel or other work. In fact, your hope is to sell quite a few books.

There are certainly ways to improve your chances of putting many of your books in front of people. Unfortunately, there are no hard statistics, no guarantees regarding what strategies work for selling many books. I can certainly share with you some of the do's and don'ts, some of the approaches that you can try and that have worked for other authors.

Let's start with the cover for your book.

You need a nice-looking, attractive one. Unfortunately, readers do judge a book by its cover. Never mind, that your story is great, that your novel is a page-turning gem. If people are turned off or less than excited by the cover, chances are they won't bother to open up your book and read that magnificent story you've written.

A cover is a potential reader's first impression while looking through the scores of books flashing on Amazon or Barnes Noble or other book sites. The book cover sets off an emotional response. Do I like what I see? Do I not like what I see? Marketing experts say that purchases are often dictated by initial positive or negative emotions.

Simply put: You need a good cover.

Now, how do you find a good, solid, eye-pleasing cover for your book?

Fortunately, there are people out there who create book covers. They can be found on sites such as Fiverr.com and 99 Designs.

You can spend a lot of money on a cover, as much as a thousand dollars or more, or pay a reasonable price for one, as low as five dollars.

From my experience, you don't have to empty out your savings account to buy a book cover. Sure, an expensive cover may get you more bang for your buck. Still, there are graphic designers who can work up a good cover quite cheaply. I've never spent any more than fifty dollars for a cover. I usually go cheaper.

If money is not an issue for you, then by all means, break the bank.

After you've decided on a budget for a cover, who will do it?

Look around. Take your time. Query several or more book cover artists. Look at the work they've done for other authors. On the Fiverr.com site this is quite easy to do. Check their ratings. How have other authors judged their work?

Does their work fit your needs? It's best to find someone who perhaps designs covers for your type of books. You probably don't want a designer who does covers for romance authors for your science fiction story.

Let's say you've selected a designer for your work. This person, we'll call him, Tim, has agreed to do your cover, for say, thirty dollars. The turn-around time is three days. You've given Tim an idea to work with for the cover for your rogue warrior novel: A fierce, muscular, gun-toting male, leading his soldiers across the battlefield.

Three days later, the cover comes back to you. It looks good, but it's not exactly what you want. Tim didn't precisely follow your directions. Maybe he forgot to include the subtitle, or the color scheme isn't quite right.

You send a message to Tim to make the proper adjustments only to learn that these costs are extra. After all, Tim carried out his part of the bargain by doing the cover in three days.

Before you have someone do a cover, make sure you know if there will be extra costs for changes. Know exactly what you're paying for before you find yourself reaching into your pocket for more money.

When the work is done, ensure the cover fits on your book. I once had a cover done that was the wrong size. Luckily, the graphic artist doing the work was happy to make the adjustments at no extra cost.

After the work is completed to your satisfaction and you approve it, you'll be asked to leave a tip—anywhere from five to fifteen dollars. Don't be afraid to tip, especially if the job was done well. Besides, you may want to use this person again for future work.

Remember, a good book cover plays a crucial part in attracting readers.

Don't just slap on any book cover.

If you self-publish through Amazon Kindle Direct Publishing, you can select from any number of templates to use for a book cover. This was the mistake I made when I first self-published my books. I'm not saying the covers were terrible, but they certainly didn't have the professional look of ones you can get done elsewhere.

For a reasonable amount of money, you can get a good cover, and it can make all the difference in helping to sell more books. A good solid cover and one that provides the reader with an idea of the book is important.

Now, who will read your book?

A reader looking for your kind of book, whether it's a mystery, a western, a biography, isn't likely to simply make a purchase after merely glancing at the cover. The description you write for your book is perhaps just as important as the cover of your book.

But how should it be written?

Good descriptions are not simply summaries. They shouldn't give away the story or the entire contents of the book. A few hundred words or more are all that is needed for a book description.

Above all, a description must grab the attention of the person scrolling through Amazon or other book sites, hopefully in that very first sentence. Remember, most of your readers are likely going to come across your books online, where the attention spans of many people are short.

Someone looking for a book to read wants to feel it's worth their time, their money. Why would they want to read your book? For pleasure or relaxation? To learn something? To solve a problem?

You need to convince the reader that your book is that very one that they want to read—for whatever reason.

Book descriptions are basically ad copy, a different kind of writing that many authors struggle with when composing their own. Not surprisingly, many authors shy away from this quite important aspect in preparing their books for publication, choosing instead to hire out copy writers to do the work for them.

You can find copy editors, including some who work cheaply and others who will charge relatively high prices.

You might want to try your hand at writing you own book description. But first, make sure you know what you're doing. Rob Eager's The Author's Guide to Write Text That Sells Books comes highly recommended by many authors.

Just to give you an idea of a book description, I'll share this one I wrote for one of my books.

Many people dream of writing a book, but few ever getting around to doing it. Why? Mike Reuther, author of Write the Darn Book, believes too many aspiring writers set themselves up for failure by believing it's difficult. It doesn't have to be. The key is writing the book from one's heart to allow for the free flow of words to come pouring out. In no time at all - a matter of weeks - a writer can have a manuscript ready to be edited and eventually published. The book also covers literary agents and the publishing world. Drawing from some of his own experience, the author reveals mistakes to avoid in writing and trying to get published. This book makes it clear that anyone with the desire to write a book can make it happen and take that first big step to become an author. And the good news is, it's quite simple. Whether one is looking to write fiction or non-fiction, the key is finding one's voice and applying the fast writing method. Write the Darn Book not only enlightens but inspires authors because it's all about writing a book from someone who's been there and done it.

In this book you will learn:

1. How to write fast
2. What to write
3. How to find your creative voice
4. Self-publishing vs. traditional publishing
5. And much more

I think it hits the high points of my book without giving everything away. Notice the four bullet points near the end of the description, each of which informs a prospective reader of the specific issues many writers face.

At less than two hundred and fifty words, it's not a lengthy description. Most people don't want to spend a long time reading through anything when looking to make book purchases.

I've sold plenty of copies of Write the Darn Book, mostly in the past year after getting better covers for the ebook and paperback versions and completely rewriting what I felt was a poor book description.

Bad Marketing

I was in a rut, not selling my books.

At least, not very many books.

I had been in this rut for quite some time.

I had tried many of the avenues out there. Maybe you know what I mean.

Tapping into social media to promote my books. Buying ads on book sites. Giving my books away for free.

Guess what happened?

Occasionally, I would see a small bump in sales for a day or two, only to find the sales soon ending.

I'd like to say that this went on for a few months, perhaps a year, before I woke up to the reality of trying something different. Instead, I retried some of these same strategies for marketing my books for years.

The hope was that as I wrote more books and promoted them as they came out, I would eventually catch lightning in a bottle. It was the old "throw enough crap at the wall and something has to stick" method.

Not that I thought my books were crappy, but ... well ... you get the picture.

Some of the reasons my books were not selling stared me right in the face. Unfortunately, I wasn't taking advantage of the successful strategies to make sales. It was easy to keep trying the same thing repeatedly. Albert Einstein said it best: The definition of insanity is doing the same thing over and over but expecting different results.

I needed to change course, to get out my own way, to apply some of these strategies that worked for other authors.

I went to the experts.

Advertising Options

I self-published for the first time in 2011 without having a clue about advertising. After uploading my mystery, Return to Dead City, into the Smashwords self-publishing platform, I waited with great anticipation to see what would happen.

In short, nothing much happened. The book sold few copies, and it soon became apparent to me that I needed to find a way to let readers know about my page-turning story about a ballplayer who turned up dead in a hotel room and the world-weary sleuth's attempts to solve the case. Smashwords was not going to do the book promotion for me.

I took a lot of the wrong approaches in attempts to sell that book and with successive books I wrote. Part of my problem was the fear of spending money on marketing. And the money I did spend was wasted on bad book promotion sites.

Don't get me wrong. There are a few book sites that can successfully put your book into the hands of readers, among them BookBub, which I will describe a bit more later. Looking back, it seems I tried them all.

Eventually, I took my first few books off the Smashwords platform and made them available exclusively through Amazon, which at the time had already become a monster in the book industry.

Each month or so, I would pick one of my books and make it available for free through Amazon's Kindle Select Program for several days, using one of the book promotions sites or a number of them to let readers know of my limited offer.

During the free offer period, I would eagerly go to my Amazon sales page to find hundreds, even a few thousand downloads of my book.

I wasn't crazy about giving my book away for nothing. The hope was that the free promotion would spark enough interest in my book to lead other people to later buy it. I usually made some sales but rarely enough to even pay for the promotion itself.

The cost of the promotions ranged from roughly twenty-five dollars to fifty dollars, so while I never lost a ton of money, they never produced for me as I had hoped.

I like to think the promotions were not a complete waste of money. After all, people were downloading my books, and in some cases, even reading them. And yet, my money could have been spent more wisely.

Often, I resorted to what I call the shotgun approach to book marketing. I'd find as many free book promotion sites as I could find and list one of my books on them. I saved money with these promotions, but I spent far too much time simply listing my book on all those sites.

Many authors agree that BookBub is probably the premiere book promotion site. BookBub's Featured Deal option can yield many sales for authors. The cost for a BookBub Featured Deal is expensive, but well worth it. If you land a Featured Deal, which is not easy, your book is guaranteed to show up before many potential readers who turn to BookBub to buy discounted books.

Amazon Ads are considered one of the best ways to market books, but they are far from a surefire method for sales. There are three kinds of Amazon Ads for authors: Sponsored Products, Lockscreen, and Sponsored Brands.

I've only done the Sponsored Products Ads. Basically, it involves the use of keywords that a reader puts into the Amazon search engine to find books. The keywords in the set-up process are selected either manually or automatically.

The manual selection allows authors to choose up to one thousand keywords—a word or several words or phrases—with bids for a particular keyword selection. The hope is that when a customer taps one of your many keywords into the Amazon search engine, your book comes up before their eyes.

Ideally, your book appears on the first page of the books listed by Amazon for that keyword, but that often requires having a high bid for the keyword.

High bids can often bring more eyes to your book but can also result in higher costs. Amazon Ads are somewhat of a gamble and require a bit of a learning curve. I don't think anyone really has a complete grasp of how the Amazon algorithms work. This is another area where a little research and learning from the experts are worth your time.

When I first delved into Amazon Ads, I was, of course, eager to sell many books, and I did see some sales. But I also lost more money than I was willing to spend because I placed too many high bids on popular and competitive keywords.

Keep your bids low for keywords. Don't bid more than say, 30 cents, and even that is perhaps too high for anyone just starting out with Amazon Ads. Check out Dave Chesson with Kindlepreneur. You can find his YouTube videos where he explains the process of using Amazon Ads. Many authors, including myself, use Chesson's Publisher Rocket tool to download keywords for their book ads.

Many authors tap into email marketing to sell books. In fact, many of the book marketing gurus out there consider email the best if not one of the best means of marketing books. Email marketing is based on the simple strategy of drawing readers through newsletters or free and discounted book offers.

Maybe you're written a book about carpentry. By building an email list of subscribers, you find potential buyers of your book through valuable information you provide.

One strategy involves using a lead magnet, often a free book offer, to keep readers interested and coming back. Mark Dawson is considered among the foremost experts on email marketing for authors. He's written books and offers podcasts on email marketing and other helpful strategies for authors.

Putting your book out there before readers is so important to sell books and there are many ways to do it. Some of the marketing strategies have been around for a long time.

I've never done a book signing, and it's not a tactic that many people suggest in these days of social media and other means of blasting products before customers. However, they can work for some authors.

Contact your local bookstore and set a date and time for you to appear and hawk your book. Some bookstores are happy to introduce that novel or other book by a local author. You show up, sit at a table, and happily talk to people who stop by to chat with you about your book. Maybe a few people you know wander into the store and see you there, surprised to learn you're an author, and shame on you for keeping it a secret.

Some authors consider book signings a waste of time, that they rarely generate much in the way of books sales. I think they are worth a try. Anything to get your name and product out there can be helpful.

If you're not a well-known author, it probably makes little sense to schedule book signings all over the map. You might sell only a few books at each location, and travel and lodging can certainly eat up your budget quite fast.

How about radio, TV, and podcast interviews? I've done a few of them, and unfortunately, I can't say they led to many book sales. But here's the thing. With rare exceptions, they are free. They're also a lot of fun. At least I think so.

What author doesn't want to yak about his or her book? Just keep in mind that the interviewer doesn't always read an author's work. In fact, I'd say most of the time they don't. I did a podcast not long ago with an amiable host who steered the conversation away from my baseball novel to talk with me about Major League Baseball.

Sure. It was fun to talk about the Mets and the Yankees and his favorite team, the Phillies, but before I knew it, the interview was over, and we had barely even talked about my book. I don't think I even had a chance to tell listeners where they could buy it.

Of course, if you can land an interview slot on a popular TV, radio or podcast with plenty of viewers or listeners, go for it.

What about word-of-mouth marketing? Sure. It works. Many of us are shy about telling everyone what a great author we are and why they must read our page-turning book, but it's a great way to let people know your novel or other work exists. Drop the fact that you are an author into conversations with people you meet. You don't have to hit them over the head with the fact or be boastful about it.

With marketing, you don't have to try everything at once. You'll be eager to sell your book, and that's understandable, but you don't want to throw a lot of money into advertising if you don't have much to spend.

Do your research. Find out how successful authors have sold books. There is no shortage of information out there about book marketing.

More times than I'd like to admit, I blasted my discounted or free books on Facebook book promotion sites only to see no return for my efforts. While it didn't cost me any money, it did result in me having my Facebook account suspended a couple of times for spamming.

Noted book marketer David Gaughran feels writers can become overwhelmed by employing too many tactics to promote books. In fact, he advises just doing one or two marketing strategies, at least when first marketing your books. Among his top three strategies are Amazon Ads, Facebook Ads and BookBub Ads.

Gaughran is also a proponent of email marketing.

Many of the marketing tactics authors try such as Twitter and Goodreads he sees as basically a waste of time. He doesn't feel radio and TV interviews do much for an author, although I have to think if you are lucky enough to secure an interview on national TV, it's nothing to bypass.

Where Should You Publish Your Book?

There is no question that Amazon is the place to be for many authors. Like it or not, Amazon is a monster, a huge online presence for customers looking for any kinds of merchandise. Books are only a piece of Amazon's vast line of products.

Amazon is likely the first platform you'll choose for selling your book, whether it's an ebook or physical copy. Most authors opt to publish both ebooks and paperbacks. And why not? Despite the rise in ebook publishing, many readers continue to buy book they can hold in their hands.

Publishing through Amazon is a fairly easy process. Basically, you upload your manuscript, cover art, and hit the publish button, although there are a few other steps to follow as well. When publishing your book, there is an option for typing keywords for your book. This is a step that should not be overlooked or ignored.

Readers use keywords to find books. The proper keywords can help sell books which is what most authors want. Unlike the Amazon Ads keywords, you don't put bid prices on these keywords. You don't have to include keywords in the setup process, but it's a mistake not to. Authors are given up to seven keywords or keyword phrases.

As with Amazon Ads, keywords should be words or phrases that potential readers are likely to type into the Amazon search engine when looking for books. If you wrote a fishing book, maybe you make fishing book or fishing books as one of your keyword phrases. As with so many aspects of book marketing, the best and most effective use of keywords have been carefully studied and analyzed.

What is your book about? Did you write a western? A mystery. Maybe a romance?

Are you planning to continue to write in that same genre? If so, you'll likely improve your chances of being successful.

You might want to consider writing a series off that first book. A series builds up a loyal readership. Think about it. A continuing story brings people back for more drama, action, suspense, and those unforgettable characters you dreamed up in your fevered imagination.

It's part of building a brand for yourself. You become known as that author who writes the cozy mysteries set in a small seaside town, that writer who pens the action adventures starring Big Al, a bounty hunter who takes on the tough, gritty underworld, risking his life and even his reputation.

Feel free to use those ideas to launch your own series.

A book series is nothing new in publishing. In years past, young readers were drawn to The Hardy Boys and Nancy Drew mysteries. There were the Max Brand westerns. My father devoured the Tarzan books by Edgar Rice Burroughs.

Self-Publishing Vs. Traditional Publishing

I tried unsuccessfully for years to become a published writer. I would write my novels then query literary agents about my book with hopes of landing a publishing deal. That was the drill in those days before self-publishing became what it is now.

Back in the day, you could self-publish, but it meant paying thousands of dollars to have copies of your book printed with the task of selling them left up to you—the author. What happened, and I guess still happens, are boxes of unsold books stacked in an author's garage and a staggering bill from the publisher.

In one of my previous books on writing, Write the Darn Book, I was careful not to bash traditional publishing. I'm not sure now traditional publishing is a good option for anyone, save an established writer or celebrity who will receive the full support of the publishing house.

Publishing has changed over the years. The unknown author who does land a publishing deal isn't likely to become rich. There exists a pecking order in traditional publishing for authors and it goes like this: Celebrity author is marketed and touted. The unknown author, not so much, if at all.

I often have wondered why authors for so many years failed to demand better treatment from traditional publishers. The monetary rewards alone should have created an uprising in the literary world. Okay. I'll step down from my soapbox.

Let's say you secure a publishing deal, likely through an agent, who by the way will likely take about fifteen percent of your royalties. You sell some books, despite the less than robust marketing plan rolled out by the publisher. Still, you're ecstatic about being a published author. Friends and strangers pat you on the back. But then reality sets in when you see how much money you do make, instead of what you feel you should be earning from your labors.

As a self-published author through Amazon you keep 70 percent of all ebook sales. For paperbacks, the earnings are a bit lower at 60 percent, but that's still a far cry above the almost criminal 10 to 12 percent in royalties that traditional publishers pay authors.

There are advantages to traditional publishing. You don't have to pay someone out of your own pocket to proofread and edit your book. Yes. The publisher takes care of the marketing, but again, unless you're a celebrity author or a big-name writer, not much time, effort and money are rolled out for an unknown author.

In the early days of self-publishing, the general consensus was that self-publishing was a haven for authors who simply didn't have the chops to be traditionally published, and I suppose there remains that stigma in some circles.

Sure, there are self-published authors who write bad, poorly written books. Not that there haven't been scores of traditionally published books that are bad as well. For the most part, the negative connotation surrounding self-publishing has vanished. Most readers who buy books don't even bother to check to see if a book is self-published.

As a self-published or independent author, you call the shots, from writing the story to deciding how to market the book. Most authors, at least when they first get into self-publishing, shudder at the very thought of having to do anything beyond writing. Marketing alone, with all the options out there, can make one's head spin.

If you really don't think you are up to the task of marketing, and choosing a cover, and finding people to edit and proofread your book, perhaps you should opt for traditional publishing. Just keep in mind, that it remains very difficult to get a publishing deal, and even if you land one, it will be a long time before your book even is ready to hit the market. Publishers are notorious for working at a snail's pace.

So, there you have it. My two cents on self-publishing versus traditional publishing. Of course, whatever route you take, you still want to write the best book you possibly can.

Self-publishing has changed since 2011, when I published my first book through Smashwords. In those days and in the next few years, before a tidal wave of self-published books hit the market, it was easier for an independent author to get noticed, to sell books.

Just because you self-publish doesn't mean the money will come rolling in from book sales. To see some degree of success you need to take care of those important details I've covered.

You can slap a bad cover on our book, refuse to edit it, and appear for all the world to be a second-rate author. You might even sell quite a few books.

But you certainly hurt your chances for many sales and building up a readership which should be one of your goals if you plan to have a future as an author and even make a living as a writer.

Do Not Give Up

It's easy to become cynical.

After you dive into this whole business of becoming an author, you may look around and see others out there doing quite well with their writing. They're earning a living with their books perhaps earning six figures a year or more.

If you're still plugging away after a few years with little to show for your efforts, you can grow weary, bitter. You wonder when your reward, your payoff, is going to come.

Before you raise the white flag, stop and think why you desired to write in the first place. It's likely you want to make some money, to be successful. If that's the case, find out what you're doing wrong. Take a good look at your books. Why aren't they selling?

Here's the thing. You're not going to learn book marketing in a week. It's a long learning curve.

Patience really is a virtue, especially for writers. Be willing to grow as an author, to learn what is needed to be successful.

There are few overnight successes in this business. It's a marathon, not a sprint.

Just Do It

I was tuned to a radio call-in program when someone queried the hosts about writing a book. The caller said he simply didn't know how to start. He was worried about grammar and syntax and basically that anything he tried to write would not be up to snuff.

The caller, an articulate man and seemingly well-educated, sounded almost desperate. He made it clear that writing was something he longed to do. And yet, he struggled just to begin the process of writing a book.

God bless the co-hosts of this program, who advised him that he need not worry about the niggling aspects of writing such as grammar and syntax. "Just get the words down on paper," he was told. "Start writing."

The caller could not have been more thankful. It was a wakeup call. He let the hosts know that it was perhaps the best piece of advice he'd ever received. He had simply been getting in his own way for far too long. He agreed he just needed to start writing.

It's this hesitation, this procrastination, that hamstrings so many people eager to get down that story they have long wanted to write. They worry that their writing will be amateurish, not up to par. So why bother? And yet, that hunger to write remains. And so, they become, like so many—frustrated, even embittered.

All writers, perhaps even the most talented authors out there, have doubts, second thoughts, perhaps even those four o'clock-in-the-morning panic attacks about their writing. It's part of being an author.

Just remember. If you're a writer, the self-doubts never completely go away.

The Natural Voice

Have you ever stopped to think how easily words tumbled out of you when you were simply messaging or emailing a friend?

With little problem at all, you dashed off a few hundred words.

Maybe you were happily recalling an event from the past or describing some weekend retreat where your families were heading that weekend.

Writing can just flow out of us when we have something we want to say, and we don't worry about the grammar police or critics.

It's writing freely and rapidly without a lot of deep thinking.

What's the best way for you?

Some authors write books by dictating the words into the computer.

To tell you the truth, I've never tried it, but it's certainly something to consider. You talk and the words appear seemingly like magic on the computer screen.

Many authors write in longhand before transcribing the words to the computer.

Still others, the real old-timers among us, bang out their words on old typewriters and wouldn't dream of taking the leap into the modern age and write on a computer.

They like that certain physical act of hitting typewriter keys and having the words appear on real paper.

The late Harlan Ellison, a prolific author of New Wave Speculative Fiction, continued to knock off his stories on a typewriter well into the Twenty-First Century. So did Larry McMurtry, author of The Last Picture Show and Lonesome Dove and many other works of fiction and nonfiction.

Before personal computers and laptops came along, typewriters were the principal tools of writers.

Whatever way you choose to get the words down, just do it.

The main thing is to be comfortable and even confident in your writing.

Maybe you're a lousy typist and take forever to tap out words.

Back when I first started writing books, I always wrote my initial drafts in longhand, but after I began to embrace the fast-writing method, I found writing in longhand to have its drawbacks. My penmanship was poor, and I had problems reading everything I had written.

And so, here I am, many years later, tapping out prose on a computer, living the writing life, the dream.

How about your writing area?

Do you have a comfortable chair?

That's important.

You'll be sitting your butt in that chair for hours and days into the future, and you don't want one that is uncomfortable or creates problems for your back or neck—an occupational hazard for many writers.

It doesn't hurt to have a place to yourself, a writing room, that is yours. This may not be possible if you live in a small house or apartment you share with family members or roommates.

Authors are known to have their own writing cottages or shacks, places away from their homes, where they escape from everyone to write. However, for most of us, that is something beyond our means.

Wherever you choose to write, make it a place you want to come to every day, a retreat where you can do what you must do—Write.

Getting in the Rhythm

Just recently, I took up downhill skiing. My second time out, I went with a friend, who has been skiing for years. I was content to spend the afternoon on the beginners' slope, but he tried to convince me that I needed to come with him to the top of one of the big hills.

Eventually, I was able to put some of my fear, my trepidations aside, and take the ski lift to the summit of a hill. From atop that mountain I looked down and I realized: Now what do I do? I had no choice but to ski down this hill, which to me appeared like a mountain in the Alps. Never mind, that we were in central Pennsylvania, where the hills are much less daunting.

As I stood on the top of that slope with my friend, where competent skiers were launching themselves down the mountain, I couldn't help but think: Now this is a little crazy.

My friend assured me that I could descend that hill too if I wasn't reckless. "Don't forget to snow-plow," he said.

Easy for you to say, I thought.

To make a long story short, I did make it down that mountain. I cheated a bit, removing my skis and walking down the steeper inclines. But hey. It was a start, no one becomes a great skier at first, and that isn't my end goal anyway.

Just remember, you won't be Hemingway (who by the way did ski) when you first start writing. Writing, unlike skiing, isn't dangerous. The only real risk is that to your ego when you think your writing sucks.

But here's the thing. When you write, you should put your ego aside. Remember. We are all different, with unique things to say. It's getting those words down on paper, letting go and allowing the chips to fall where they may.

But don't I need a degree in writing, perhaps a class in creative writing, to even think about beginning to write a book?

The short answer to that question is a resounding No. On the other hand, there is certainly nothing wrong with studying writing and learning some of the rudiments of what makes a good story. You can join a writing group, find a mentor, go on YouTube sites and Podcasts to listen to authors talk about how to write. You can glean a lot of information from countless sources about writing a book.

Just don't spend months or even years gathering information without getting yourself in front of that keyboard and writing. Don't use the excuse that you're not quite ready to begin because you don't know enough about the craft of writing a book.

Writing, like so many pursuits, is best learned by doing. Again, the more you do it, the better you'll become. Be a writer, not a watcher. Get off the beginners' slope and take the plunge down that big hill. Fear of failure is perhaps the greatest sin of writers. And as I've mentioned previously, the most successful writers are those who are persistent, not the ones with the most talent.

Be persistent, be confident, and not afraid. Write the book you've always wanted to write.

What have you got to lose?

I Got My Writing in Today

Six words. I ... got ... my ... writing ... in ... today.

You don't even need to say that sentence aloud. It will run through your brain each a day you carry out the task of writing.

Those words will feel good, give you satisfaction. As they should. And if you continue putting yourself in front of that keyboard every day and tapping out words, you'll find yourself developing a habit—a good habit. That feeling of satisfaction will be part of your life.

Sure. Life happens. Things get in the way. It can become easy to put the writing aside.

Maybe you're dealing with unpleasant personal or work problems. Write anyway. Few things in life are as satisfying as getting that work done every day.

Writing is a journey. The book you're writing now or plan to write will be in the past. You'll move on to other writing projects. Other stories will follow. You'll grow older, have more experiences, perhaps have a different outlook on life.

And so, you write some more. The years go by and you've written ten, twenty, thirty books. Think it's impossible? Think again.

A thousand words a day. That's seven thousand words a week. Thirty-thousand words a month. There's a short novel right there. And really, that's a modest output. Many authors crank out multiple books a year, some of them driven by the demands of a readership eager to buy their books, perhaps the different stories that comprise a series.

Some people knock off entire books in a weekend. Yes. There are workshops and seminars out there for writers to do just that. I never tried it, but it's something to consider.

Fast writing is natural writing, unencumbered by doubts and misstarts and too much thinking. It's getting into the flow and letting it all go.

I believe it's the best way to write.

But getting the writing done. That's what's important. Set your course and begin. Are you ready for the journey?

Maybe you need support. Find a mentor, another writer. Talk to other people who write books. Join a writing group. Maybe you tried that and didn't like the people in the group. They were snarky and hypercritical. The hell with them. Join another group.

Support is a great thing for a writer. After all, writing can be lonely. It's likely you're the only person in your circle of friends who wants to write a book. You may not personally know anyone who's ever written a book.

That doesn't mean it's wrong, odd, silly, or some phase you're going through. Besides, who wants to be like everyone else? You're a writer with dreams and goals and a burning desire to create.

What more can I say?

Now get to it.

I Really Want to Write

Who knows why you want to write? Maybe a certain book you read lit a hot creative fire. Perhaps the sheer joy of stringing words together or telling a story excites you. There's a story or many stories inside just dying to get out.

The reason doesn't matter.

You were that smart girl, the head of your high school class, who went to an Ivy League School. When you graduated, the future looked bright—a solid career with high earnings. But you wanted to write instead. That time working on the school newspaper got you to thinking: I like to write, but I can't make much money as a writer, and definitely not as a novelist.

Maybe you were that other person, someone from an impoverished home, perhaps a high school dropout. Your options in life are few. It's either work at some miserable job or life on the streets. Some of your best times were hanging out in the local library reading books by authors such as Thomas Pynchon or Don Delillo. You've always been kind of a dreamer, and now you're thinking you want to write. In fact, lately you've found yourself scribbling out words on paper, perhaps imitating the prose of Pynchon or Delillo. You want to write but don't know how to start.

Chances are you're not much different from a lot of people. You have a job, a circle of friends, a hobby or two you enjoy, a comfortable enough life, but you must write—for whatever reason.

You have an important story to write: Your struggle with drugs or mental illness.

I had a lot of reasons for wanting to write a book. I longed to create, to be heard, to see my name on a book and have people read it. The idea of not writing a book seemed unacceptable. And yet, I waited until I was thirty years old before I started doing it.

Not that thirty is old, but I really didn't need or want to wait that long.

It's never too young or too old to start writing. Maybe you've read through this book, and you still don't feel ready. Maybe you're too busy or the desire to write simply isn't that strong.

Perhaps you can't foresee spending much time doing anything if there is no guarantee of a monetary reward. If that's the reason, you probably shouldn't write. There are no guarantees that anything any author writes will yield riches.

So if you've decided that writing a book is a silly notion, that you're better off doing something else with your time, starting a business, going off to graduate school, volunteering, bicycling across America, then by all means don't become an author.

But guess what? There is a good chance that that itch to write will continue to hound you.

Only you can decide if writing a book is worth trying. Is it a leap of faith? Well ... yes. Just remember. Writing a book doesn't cost any money. The only thing you are really giving up is a piece of your time on this earth.

Let's say you decide to write a book and you finish it. Think of the accomplishment. Think how you will feel. You set out to do something not many people have done, something you didn't know you could do.

Or you could start a book and quit. Will that mean you're a failure? Hardly. Even an attempt at writing a book is something few people have done.

Maybe you begin a book and quit and realize you're not a writer after all. Is that what you fear?

The other option, of course, is not writing at all. Giving up before you even try. The world is full of people who never get off the sidelines, who refuse to give something a shot for fear of embarrassment or failure.

There you have it. The choice is up to you. Every author, even the most celebrated ones, faced that fear of setting down words for a book for the first time.

The fears, the apprehensions, exist. You must move past the fears and write anyway. You don't have to know exactly where you're going when you sit down to write every day. So much of writing is trusting your instincts, turning on the faucet and letting the words flow.

There are road maps for so many things we do in life. And that's fine. Writing is a craft but also an art. As writers, we have unique voices and thoughts and emotions that we put into our stories. There is no wrong path to take when we write a book. Not really. Oh sure. There are bad books, which are poorly crafted, a jumbled mess of words that amount to nothing.

Is that what you fear? Writing a horrible book? And if so, do you fear it will stop you from ever attempting to write a book again?

Put aside the fears, the idea that only the few, the chosen, can write books. Don't sit around wanting to write and not doing it. Don't give up the dream.

When you go to bed tonight, set your alarm clock for a time in the morning when you'll wipe the sleep from your eyes get yourself in front of that computer or writing tablet to start writing. Set that alarm for the same time every morning for your time to write.

Get in the habit of writing. Find your rhythm, your groove, which is so important for a writer. Keep at it long enough and you'll find it harder to stop writing than to start writing. In fact, the idea of missing more than a day or two of writing will fill you with dread, and that's when you know you are well on your way to becoming an author.

Once again, the fears, the apprehensions, will never completely go away. It's simply part of being a writer. Accept the fears and press on. Try not to miss a writing day, but if you do, forget about it, and write the next day.

You're not Superman. Nobody is. You're a writer, and that's a damn fine creature to be.

The End

87

The following is an excerpt from Mike Reuther's book, Writing Fiction, Telling Tales.

Chapter 1

If you want to write a novel, what's stopping you?

Really? What's stopping you?

To tell you the truth, it's one of the easiest things to do.

I know what you're thinking. How can this guy say that? I mean, I've wanted to write the book of my dreams for a long time, and he's saying I can easily do it.

Well ... you can.

But if you're like a lot of people, you're getting hung up on those nagging questions: How should I start my book? Is it worth writing? Will anyone ever read it? And I suppose these are all legitimate questions. I had some of these same feelings when I started out with dreams of writing my novels and even well after I began banging out stories.

Writing fiction is reaching into your soul and telling the story you want to tell. It's writing that mystery, that romance novel, that western that you've long wanted to share with the world.

No one is forcing you to write. It's not a job, where you're expected to be at your desk or cubicle or behind the wheel of a truck at an appointed time to perform a certain amount of work. No one is paying you to write a book. You don't have to do it. For many of us, that's a big reason it's so hard to write a book. You simply do not have to do it.

There's no guarantee you'll make any money writing a book. In fact, it's highly likely you'll make hardly any money at all. Of course, in this new era of ebook publishing, you can at least get your work out there before readers with little problem at all. But again, with no assurance of a great monetary reward awaiting you, it's easy to forget about this whole crazy notion of writing a book.

Why should anyone invest any time at all into writing a book, let alone a novel? That's a very good question. You don't need to write. No one does. If you want to write a book, you should burn with the desire to do it.

Ask yourself the following questions: Are stories forever swirling in your brain? Do you ever read a book and think you could tell a better story than the author? Do you like to put words to paper and see how they look on a page and how the words sound when you read them out loud? Is the written word something you cherish? Are you a voracious reader who loves nothing better than a good tale?

Here's a tip. Those nagging feelings of whether to write a book aren't likely to soon vanish. Believe me, I know. Dismiss those feelings if you like. Chalk them up to silly notions or a middle-aged crisis if you must. But they're real.

Look around you. What do you see? Chances are you have friends, acquaintances, co-workers who don't care a whit about books. Perhaps no one you know has ever wanted to write a book. The world is not particularly kind to the artist, the creative person. Oh sure, we celebrate great works of art, novels such as Gone with the Wind and plenty of other stories that have been made into films. But those are exceptions. Most creative works, be they paintings, novels scribbled out by writers, are ignored. Their creators toil in relative anonymity - unknown, uncelebrated.

Most of us are not encouraged to pursue a life in the arts. Oh, a creative outlet of some kind is fine as a hobby, but it's better to go to college and study business administration or engineering or something practical. You simply won't be able to make a living as a writer. At least, that's the general consensus.

When I was a young guy, I wanted to write the great American novel. It was a lofty ambition to be sure. However, for the longest time I did nothing about trying to realize that dream. Oh, I kind of had a plan, and it went like this: I'd study journalism in college, graduate from school, find a job with a newspaper, work for a few years to sharpen my writing skills, and then get down to the real task of writing fiction.

When you're in your mid-twenties with the rest of your life ahead of you, and the passion of youth is burning inside you like a red-hot flame, anything seems possible.

Unfortunately, I needed a wake-up call, as many of us do, before I started to write my first novel. And boy did I get one. The small-town newspaper where I was working not so very happily was sold to a larger company intent on changes. I was let go from my job, fired, along with many other people.

Just like that, I had all this time on my hands. Time to write. On a Thanksgiving night I picked up a pen and opened a notebook to begin the story that had long percolated inside my head for so many years, a coming-of-age novel that I simply had to write. And so, I wrote, carefully scribbling out my words in longhand before later typing my story on an old manual typewriter. Hey. This was the late 1980s folks. Most people didn't have home computers. In a couple of years, I tried without success to have it published. But of course, it was the usual story of a first-time author being rejected by countless literary agents.

That's the way it used to be. Writers had no choice but to repeatedly send out letters to agents - the gatekeepers to the publishing houses - hoping, praying that one would sign them to contracts and find them those elusive book deals. It was oh so difficult to get published in those days. Traditional publishers rarely took on new authors. As a matter of fact, it continues to be hard for authors to land lucrative publishing deals. Times have changed, of course. With the revolution of epublishing, writers can now get their works into print quite easily.

But for many years, I was going up against that world, a kind of David pit against Goliath, yet determined to somehow become a published author. I felt deep in my heart that I was meant to be an author. I didn't want to do anything else.

I held a job, raised a family, lived a life not unlike many people, but I still found time to write. There was no guarantee that all the time I spent writing was going to ever pay off. Still, I wrote and dreamed and hoped that I would be a published author. And it finally happened, thanks to epublishing and print on demand.

With epublishing and print on demand services, a writer no longer must worry about never being published. Now, anyone can write a book and have it out there flashing on Amazon's pages. I'm thankful for these relatively new trends in publishing. They've given me a chance to be published, to finally have my books out there before readers. Epublishing and print on demand have thrown open the door to new writers. No longer does traditional publishing control the book world.

What's stopping so many of you from getting started writing that novel? That mystery? That creepy horror story that will make readers forget Stephen King?

About the Author

Mike Reuther is the author of the Amazon bestselling book, Nothing Down, as well as other novels and books on writing. A journalist, baseball nut and flyfisherman, he makes his home with his family in central Pennsylvania near some of his favorite trout streams.